Wire Wrapping Book for Beginners

Learn How to Craft 20 Bead Making Jewelry
Designs and Projects with Step by Step Instructions,
Plus Tools and Techniques to Get You Started

By

Gina Bowen

Disclaimer

This publication is designed to provide competent and reliable information regarding the subject matter covered. However, the views expressed in this publication are those of the author alone, and should not be taken as expert instruction or professional advice. The reader is responsible for his or her own actions.

The author hereby disclaims any responsibility or liability whatsoever that is incurred from the use or application of the contents of this publication by the purchaser or reader. The purchaser or reader is hereby responsible for his or her own actions.

Table of Contents

Introduction

Wire-wrapping is a technique that involves folding, twisting, wrapping and then, cutting wire strands to make ornate pieces of jewelry and ornaments. You'd be surprised at how simple the art is. In fact, it is the simplicity of it that made it stay accepted till today. Of course, some machines make jewelry, so us choosing to make it with our hands instead can only mean that there is fun in it. You don't need to buy machines or get any part of the strings soldered. All you need are a well of creativity, a few basic tools and your hands! In fact, the more work or techniques you can achieve with your hands, the better your project will be because there will virtually be no scratch marring it.

However, you'd still need to learn the skill, no matter how simple it looks or sounds. That's why this book, **Wire-Wrapping Book for Beginners** was made. It contains every necessary detail that you will need. A few of them include techniques, tricks, tips, safety measures, principles that will guide you on how to set your workshop, and many more. Then, most importantly, you have twenty loaded projects that will guide you on how you can make the finest ornaments.

So, what are you still waiting for? Delve into this art with me, while gripping your favorite cookie in your free hand!

Chapter 1

Basics of Wire Wrapping

What is a Wire Wrapped Jewelry?

Wire-wrapped jewelry is an ornate material that is made by twisting, turning, cutting, and hammering metal strings. Most times, the art is used to create ornaments like bracelets, anklets, rings, necklaces, and so on. For this art, all you need for a successful project is a very flexible string whose shape or structure can be easily altered by pliers or by your fingers. This art is unique because the materials you need for it are cheap and readily available. You also do not need additional procedures like soldering, gluing, or heating of the metallic string. The projects are usually braced or supported with solid twists and windings, so you would see that this is one reason they can remain the way they are for years without their shape being altered.

Jewelry made with this hand-made technique is usually produced on a small scale as the system does not work much for large scale production. There are machines for that purpose. So here, you mostly use your fingers to bend and twist craft wires to get jewelry. The wire strings are usually bent into loops and other ornate ties that support or bear other twisted components. The ability of a wire string to bent into any shape is measured by gauge numbers. Wire strings with a gauge number of 16 will be very hard to twist. The ones with numbers like 18 will be relatively softer. Numbers like 22 and 24 mark very thin wire strings. So, the higher the gauge number of a wire string is, the softer and thinner it is. To spice up things, you could add beads, water crystals, pendants, or aquamarine stones to the wire strings. So, the name wire-wrapping was coined from the techniques the art involves which is the principle of wrapping a wire string about another.

History of Wire Wrapping

Wire-wrapping is one of the ancient arts that ever existed. This art is one that does not need soldering or any other thermal process to melt wire strings, so it was quite easy to follow through with it. Then, in the olden days, the people then used wire-wrapped jewelry for decoration, identification and several other remarkable purposes. The use of this principle dates back to about 1440BC, which is a very long time ago. At first, the early men made pieces of jewelry by threading teeth, bones, pearls, and shells through steins of twine or sinew gotten from animals. It was later that the use of metal strings came into being. When researches were made recently, a few of the materials used for the art were found in several pyramids in Egypt. Luckily, for record purposes, the metal strings used did not decompose or get destroyed over time.

Then, the metal strings were obtained from sheets of metal that were subject to continuous hammering. After that, the then flattened sheets were then cut into strips which were, in turn, rolled into strings. Sulfur would then be used to strengthen the strings of wire. These strings were soft and flexible enough to turn and twist into several beautiful projects. The only thing that caused his art to remain accepted by the craft world even after the advent of technology and machines is its simplicity. You don't need to solder or subject the metal sheets to any form of heat. All you need us to just twist and cut, then, you've got your jewelry.

In the British Museum, you'd see pieces of jewelry that were wrapped manually in periods as far behind as the Sumerian dynasty that is based in the cemetery of Ur. Some other wire-wrapped projects were also found in Rome's ancient cities. In this country especially, wire-wrapping was favored because it was a quick and intricate way of producing strong pieces of jewelry. So, since then, many more people have laid their hands on the skill, even to the point where the younger generation are now encouraged to try their hands on it.

Wire Wrapping Safety Tips

1. Do not wrap wires without using safety goggles. Wire strings are thin and can easily poke your eyes if you are not too careful. The probability of this incident happening is greater now that the craft is something you do with your hands and eyes close to the strings. Also, as you use your flushing tool to trim the excess wire strings as you cut, there's a high tendency it flies in a tangent directed towards your eye. Be careful.

2. If you will be using certain pigments for your work, see that you wear aprons or overalls. Some resins work to leave terrible stains on your clothes and you'd certainly not like them.

3. Here, you will be handling needles, pliers, and a lot of other heavy equipment like hammers. See that you never walk barefooted in your workplace or go up and down with a pair of

sandals. Fully covered shoes with thick leather bodies are much more preferable.

4. Since you will be working with beads too, check their make-up to see that they ate not coated with flammable chemicals. If they are, keep them from fire and heat.

5. You should also try to keep your equipment arranged in boxes. Keep the needles in one place, the beads in another, and so on, to keep your workplace orderly.

Chapter 2

Terms Used in Wire Wrapped Jewelry

The following terms are some of the words that you will come by in the world of wire-wrapping. You should try to acquaint yourself with them and what they mean.

1. **Bolt clasp:** This clasp is shaped into circles. It has a spring within its structure that is tied to a bolt that you can control with your fingernail before the springs close.

2. **Cabochon**: A cabochon is a gemstone that is cut out in a way that its back is flat and the top is rounded. You would see that most cabochon gemstones usually have smooth, and polished surfaces. Their upper surfaces could also be cut out in rose-cuts.

3. **Casting**: This term describes the process of producing metallic instruments. Here, the molten form of the metal is poured into a mold where it lies and stiffens into cold and compact metal. You could either cast with sand or with centrifuges.

4. **Chasing**: This term is achieved with a chasing hammer. It has two kinds of edges—the flat end and the rounded end. You use this tool to change the shape of metal and to impact a particular kind of texture to the hammered metal.

5. **Chandelier**: This term is attributed to designs. They have metallic frameworks that can be used to hold up different kinds of beads. This kind of design is usually employed when constructing exquisite earrings, and pendants.

6. **Cocktail ring**: This kind of ring has a large focal point at the top of the center of a band. These are the kinds of rings you wear once in a while because of their big sizes.

7. **Crimp bead**: This bead is used to fasten the knotted ends of a necklace. You'd use pliers to press this bead to keep it in place on a wire string.

8. **Cultured pearls**: These pearls are made by farmers under closely monitored conditions. To get them, you could look for mollusks that live in freshwater habitats or the pearl oysters that stay in saltwater habitats.

9. **Ear wire**: This is constructed from wire that you'd use to pierce ears. A common type of ear wire

available is Shepherd's hook whose focal point projects from the upper surface of the wire. Ear wires are also referred to as ear hooks.

10. **Emerald cut:** Stones cut with this technique usually have the shape of rectangles and squares. You'd employ this technique when making big and transparent gemstones.

11. **Faceted gemstone:** This gemstone has the shape of a diamond. The upper part has several edges and behind its structure is a central point. Faceted gemstones are set into claw shapes. Cabochons can also be cut using this technique.

12. **Freshwater pearls:** These kinds of pearls are gotten from freshwater mollusks. These pearls can be in different kinds of shapes and they are not as costly as pearls gotten from saltwater regions.

13. **Gauge:** This is a term used to measure the density of a wire string. In the world of jewelry, the kind of wire gauge you need could range from 4g to 34g. The smaller the gauge is, the more the diameter will be.

14. **Jump ring:** This ring is used to connect clasps, pendants, beads, and ear wires. They are small in size but are commonly used decorative tools.

15. **Lobster clasp:** This type of clasp is firm with claws that are shaped like a lobster. They also have tiny springs within the clasps with which you handle the clasp. Lobster clasps can also be referred to as parrot or carabineer clasps. You'd utilize this clasp when making pieces of jewelry like the Simone Walsh necklace.

16. **Mother-of-pearl:** This pearl has the kind of coating you would find within the inner shells of an oyster. You would need this bead to create beads and pendants.

17. **Rondelle:** This term describes a bead that is flatter at the top than it is at the bottom. So, instead of having a round shape, it comes out in form of a doughnut. These kinds of beads could either have smooth or faceted edges.

18. **Sterling Silver:** This is a specialized type of Silver that is as fine as four hundred and twenty-five portions per five hundred portions of silver. Then, it has about seventy-five components of copper out of a figure of 1000. These added

components only work to make the silver tougher.

Chapter 3

Wire Wrapping Tips and Tricks

1. When stringing small beads or gemstones, you can work with a wire of 6mm diameter.
2. When creating jump rings or findings, you could work with wire strings of 0.8mm to 1mm diameter.
3. When creating rings, bangles, and bracelets, you should work with strings with diameters that range between 2mm and 3mm.
4. Wire-wrapping is a technique that majorly involves the wrapping of wires. So, thick wire strings may be hard to manipulate. When that happens, all you need to do is heat the wire and then cool it, while following that succession repeatedly.
5. To prevent the wire strings from cutting through your skin, always ensure that you file the ends of the wire with flat files or needle files. You could also trim the excess strings with a flush cutter

before tucking in whatever is left within the whorls of the twisted wire string.

6. Round-loop pliers are one of the tools that you will mostly need for wire-wrapped jewelry. They are used to create loops in wire strings, so it is very helpful if you kept them close to you.

7. After wrapping your wire strings, see that you keep your wire strings hard and strong. You can achieve this technique by hammering the strings on a bench block with a chasing hammer, by twisting the strings with your pliers, or by tugging repeatedly at the strings until they are straight enough. A hardened wire string is not readily worn out as it has the inner strength required to keep its form.

8. When you feed gemstones into a loop, ensure that you close up the loop with a pair of pliers.

9. Round-nose pliers and dowels are the tools you would need to create regular loops in a wire string before you head on to shape it. To make these loops, fix the mouth of the pliers at the point you want the loop to be in. At this point, see that the mouth is open. Then, hold the end of the wire string with your fingers before you twist the

wire string about the round-nose pliers' jaw. Afterward, you can make the rest loops with your fingers.

10. Some wire wrapping techniques involve you gripping the bottom of the wires with the tips of your forefingers. So, to prevent a situation where your fingers get cramped up at the joints, you could use a ring clamp. To use them, you'd wear them around your fingers before attaching the strings to them. However, you might need to regularly adjust it so that the length of the weave above the clamp is not more than ½ inch.

11. To prevent a scenario where the wire strings uncoil from the spool you wound them about much faster than you work with it, see that you position the spool on the floor. This way, the wires will also not become tangled as you work with them.

12. Before you work on expensive wire strings like the Sterling silver wire, ensure that you try out the cheap ones. This way, your mistakes won't be too costly.

13. Try to avoid reaching out for a wire-wrapping tool every single time. Most of the things can be

done with your fingers. If you took time to study, you'd see that twists made with the fingers are neater and more intricate.

14. Do not allow your fingers to run along the wire strings from causing your skin to become sore or red. To avoid this issue, you can cover your fingers with fabric tape. This kind of tape will not hinder the easy flow of the strings between your fingers.

15. To prevent knots from forming along the length of your wire strings, keep it straight. If you see any knot, go back to loosen it before continuing. Bear in mind that knots will only weaken a rope.

16. When coiling a string of rope around a mandrel, always see that you press the coils together with your fingers. Do not allow the rings of the coil to either overlap or have too much space between them.

17. Store your silver jewelry in plastic bags so that it can retain its gleam. Silver is easily affected or destroyed by chlorine and sunlight, so try to shield them from those elements as much as possible.

18. See that you have anti-tarnish strips in your jewelry box. You can easily use these strips for about three to six months before you eventually throw them out.

19. You can regain the lustrous look of your pearls by washing them as often as possible in warm soapy water. Pearls are very fragile, and so, you should award them more care than you would do your other beads.

20. You can preserve a Swarovski crystal best by immersing it in a mix of mild soap and water. Afterward, you can then wrap the crystal in a dry damp towel to get rid of the fluid.

A Short message from the Author:

Hey, I hope you are enjoying the book? I would love to hear your thoughts!

Many readers do not know how hard reviews are to come by and how much they help an author.

I would be incredibly grateful if you could take just 60 seconds to write a short review on Amazon, even if it is a few sentences!

>> Click here to leave a quick review

Thanks for the time taken to share your thoughts!

Chapter 4

Getting Started with Wire-Wrapping

Now that you have known what the concept of wire-wrapping is about and what it entails, it is time to get dirty and get started with the preliminary things needed to make your first wire wrapping project. First, we will take a look at all the equipment and materials you will need to start your wire-wrapping projects. Then, you will also be acquainted with their purposes and mode of operations. However, to make this stage as sweet as possible, endeavor to learn the terms we discussed earlier. They will begin to show up more frequently from here.

Basic Tools and Materials

Wire

Under this material, we will take a deep look at the concept of gouges and wire shapes. However, know that the best wire you can get is one that is flexible enough to be looped or twisted, and at the same time not susceptible to breakage.

The gauge of any wire is a measurement of its internal diameter. You'd see the abbreviation, 'ga' beside any gauge dimension. It is also a term that is characterized by the number of times a wire string is fed through a draw plate before you begin to get it sized. The more times you feed a wire string through a draw plate, the thinner it will get. Now, let's take a look at a few gauge dimensions.

- **32-28ga:** Wire strings that fall into this class are very thin and can only be employed for delicate wire weave projects like crotchet, and Viking knits.
- **26-24ga:** The wire strings in this class are fed through pearls and beads that have small holes. Wire strings with this gauge number can also be used for Viking knits.
- **22-20ga**: The strings in this glasswork for all purposes. They are thin enough to be fed through the opening of most beads. Besides, they are strong enough to retain their shape and can be used to make chains, ear wires, eye pins, jump rings, lightweight clasps, and so on. They would also be perfect to make necklaces and bracelets.

- **18-16ga**: The strings in this category are for making clasps and jump rings. You could use the strings in this category to make clasps for your ornaments, as well as jump rings. With this technique, you can make necklaces as well as bracelets. The 18ga wire is great for ear hooks. The 16ga wire's strength depends on the kind of metal it was cut out from.

- **14ga**: The strings in this class are used for projects that require a high degree of strength. This is because the strings are relatively thick and so, are perfect for ornaments like clasps, rings, cuff bracelets, bangle bracelets, etc. You could also use the string in this class as a means of support.

- **12ga**: The strings in this class are great for making ornaments that will frame the neck, fingers, and wrists. They can be found in dead soft making. To cut through this string, you might need to get a jeweler's saw.

- **10ga**: This string is good for cuff ornaments. To cut through this string or even get it shaped, you will need a jeweler's saw.

Now, the next thing to consider is the various shapes wire strings exist in. The wire shape being referred to here is the cross-sectional area of the string.

- **Round wire:** This is the shape in which the majority of the wire strings exist in. They are used for several wire-wrapping projects.
- **Square wire:** You should get wires with this shape for designs that require embellishments. The only issue with this wire string is that it may be hard to bring several wire strings together because of the flat edges.
- **Half-round wire:** This wire is the wire that is used to link several pieces of square wires. This technique of joining the square wires is known as banding.
- **Twisted wire:** This wire offers both decorative and textural qualities to the wire string. You can get it from either a round wire or a square wire string. You twist wire strings yourself, you could make use of pin vises.

Beads

The kind of beads you need for wire-wrapping just depends on whether or not the opening is wide enough for wire strings to pass through. However, for more intricate and sophisticated projects, you could also pay attention to this section. Let's see the different kinds of beads you can come across and their uses.

- **Gemstone beads**

These kinds of beads are also referred to as semi-precious beads. Gemstone beads aren't totally made from gemstones. They are infiltrated with some synthetic gemstones too. You would readily find gemstones in various sizes of 4mm, 6mm, 8mm, 10mm, and even 12mm.

- **Natural pearls and shells**

These beads are gotten from salt-water and fresh-water aquatic habitats. You could find them pink, peach, white, or even creamy. It is the pearls gotten from the water bodies that are then cut into beads.

- **Wooden beads**

For this type of wood, you can work with plaques sourced from grey wood, jack fruit, oak wood, rosewood, and palm wood.

- **Crystal beads**

The beads in this category are made from leaded glass that has a high degree of luster. For an even improved shine, they have several glinting sides and the commonest of these crystals is the Swarovski. The Czech crystals are also good, but cheaper.

- **Bugle beads**

The beads here have the shape of a tube. They are usually cut out into different sizes. These beads belong to the group of seed beads, so you can work with them when creating intricate jewelry. They are available in sizes 0.5, 1, 1.5, 2, 3, 5, etc. The first dimension is the shortest available.

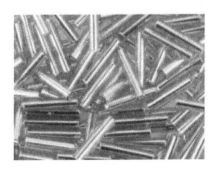

- **Delica beads**

These beads are small and have the shape of a cylinder. They are thin-walled beads with large openings. Delicate beads can be available in two different sizes. There is size 11 and also, size 8. The latter is known as the double Delica. You can use this bead for intricate beadwork sequences and designs.

- **Faceted beads**

These kinds of beads have several flat sides and edges that give out a radiant effect as if it is constructed from glass. Examples include Rondelles.

- **Rondelles**

These beads are smaller than the usual round beads, and so, they can be easily used as a spacer. You'd find them in all finished forms and sizes.

- **Seed beads**

These beads are short pieces of chopped glass rods that are heated until you get smoothly curved shapes.

- **Rocaille or round beads**

You'd find these beads mostly in sizes 15 and 3. Contrary to your thoughts, size 3 is bigger than the size 3 round bead. You would use round beads for beadwork projects and as spacers.

Flush Cutters

This is a tool that is used for cutting through wire strings that are used for making pieces of jewelry. This tool has one leveled and smooth edge with the other side laid with bevels that make it sharp. You would use this tool to cut off every excess of wire from your wire-wrapping projects.

Pliers

There are different kinds of pliers employed for wire-wrapping as given below.

- Round-nose pliers.

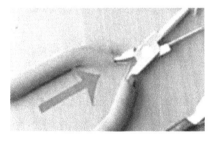

This tool has two jaws shaped in form of a cone. It is used for making loops along the length of wire strings. Rosary pliers also do the same thing this tool does. The only difference is that the rosary pliers have one round jaw and another cutting jaw.

- Chain-nose pliers

The jaws are regular and smooth at the internal surfaces. However, they have a narrow mouth that can be used to grasp and bend a wire string into a curve.

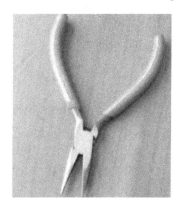

- Bent-chain nose pliers.

This tool is bent in comparison to the ordinary chain-nose pliers. This additional feature is what makes you able to wrap wires for a long time without having your wrists begin to hurt.

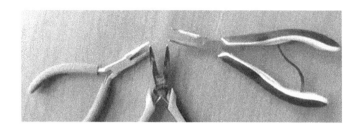

- Jaw pliers

There are two types of jaw pliers. There are the nylon jaw pliers that have their jaws shielded with nylon. This shield will prevent your wire strings from being stretched unnecessarily by the tool as you use it. So, jaw pliers are used for straightening wire strings.

The other type is the step-jaw pliers. One of the jaws is smooth and the other jaw has three cylindrical steps with varying sizes. The smallest jaw is at the uppermost side of the jaw whole the biggest side is at the bottom.

Ruler

Rulers are used for taking wire length readings, bead diameter readings, and other readings tied to jewelry.

Permanent Marker

This tool is used to mark wire strings at certain points before you cut through them or bend them.

Files

Files are used to make the sharp ends of a cut wire string smooth and regular. They act like sandpapers and leave the edges round. An example of a file used for this purpose is the cup bur. It is a specialized file that rounds the end of a wire string. There is usually one small groove inside it. This groove is lined with a filing surface that acts like sandpaper.

Chasing Hammer

This kind of hammer has two edges. One is flat and the other one is round. It is used to harden a project after you are done, especially with ones involving swirls and hooks. To get smooth finishes, you should hammer your project with a flat sound. To give your projects a rougher look, hit it with the round side.

Steel Bench Block

This tool is tied with the chasing hammer. This is the platform on which you place your project before you begin to hit it.

Mandrels

This is the tool you will need to set your ornate project into a particular shape. It has a long handle with a smooth and regular surface that does not scratch the material you use for it. If you want to make rings, you would need a ring mandrel. Ring mandrels have the same size as the regular rings you wear. So, when you use them, the rings retain the shape they were in before you began the process, and most importantly, still keep on being round.

Metal Hole Punch

These punches are the things that help to drive things like nails and dowels through a surface. They could even make dents so minor that they could be strung together as images or sequences.

Beading Needles

Beading needles are used to thread small beads together. There are several kinds of bead weaving techniques in a jewelry project.

- The English Beading needle, which can thread any kind of bead.
- The Japanese beading needle, which can help to remove split ends from a wire.
- Big eye needles with an opening that runs down the whole length of the needle.
- Twisted beading needles that are very easy to thread.

Crimp Tool

This tool is used to join two strings of wire for jewelry projects. You can also use it to finish clasps or insert crimp beads into your projects.

Jigs

A jig is a platform with holes and metallic pegs that fit into them. This tool is used to make a connection between the different wire components of your project. There is the Wig Jig Centaur, the Wig Jig Delhi. The two have metallic pegs that are about 1/16 inches long. Then, each peg should be at a distance of 5holes per inch. This way, you can make more intricate jewelry. The Wig Jig centaur is a mix of the square peg arrangement and the round arrangements of wig jigs. The round sequence of the wig jig centaur is one that increases from the top of the platform while going round at an angle of thirty degrees. So, any necklace or ornament you make with this tool will dangle in a semi-circular shape around your neck.

Setting Up a Jewelry Workshop At Home

Getting a room ready for the execution of your wire-wrapping projects is one of the essential things we are going to consider. First, you need to get a safe area that won't give you issues as you work. Since you will be handling a lot of metallic tools, you need to consider the issue of rust. Metal rust is caused by exposure of a metallic surface to moisture. So, you have to ensure that the room you work in is not so damp that your working tools get affected adversely.

Next, before you choose a place, see that the room is well illuminated. Light is very important for your project to be run smoothly. You could also try getting LED lamps, desk lamps, or LED headbands with a light attached. Now that you have settled the issues related to a working space, you can move ahead to construct a workbench. Well, you could purchase one too if you have the funds. Just ensure that the bench is such that you don't have to crane your neck too upwards or downwards. Apart from that, you could get a workbench with drawers and compartments where you can store things in.

The seat you get should be one that can be readily readjusted. It should support your back and your neck as you work to prevent you from complaining of aches thereafter. The seat should also not be higher than your workbench.

Next, gather all the necessary and basic equipment and see that they are stacked in the right storage boxes. Decorate your walls with a few charts and your projects too so that anyone that comes in can have an idea of what you do. Then, you should consider getting basic things like first aid boxes and fire extinguishers too.

Wire Wrapping Jewelry Techniques

There are several techniques that you need to first learn, which will help you in making some of the projects that will be discussed in the next chapter. Here, we will look at a few of the crucial ones.

Making a P-loop

1. Use round-nose pliers to grip one side of your wire strings. See that there's a bit of excess wire away from the side the jaw of the plier is gripping.
2. Grip your pliers with one end, and then, use the thumb of your other hand to pass the wire across the jaws of your pliers. Ensure that your thumb is as close as possible to the pliers' jaws.
3. This way, you will get a P-shaped loop at the end of the wire string.

Straightening wire strings

1. When you get wire strings, you'd notice that they have a somewhat bent structure. So, before you use it for your projects, you have to straighten it.
2. Cut out a particular length of the wire string, then, create a loop at its end.
3. You can straighten the wire by gripping the loop and then, have it dragged through the jaws of the nylon-jaw pliers repeatedly.
4. Grip the handles of the pliers with one hand and then, press it on each length of the wire string. Then, use your other hand to tug at the loop (at the end of the wire) with your thumb and forefinger.

Bending wire strings

You would need to bend most wire strings through an angle of ninety degrees for most projects.

1. First, grip the wire string with bent chain nose pliers, while ensuring that the mouth of the tool is right at the point where the wire string is to be bent.

2. Use one hand to grip the pliers and the thumb of the other to push at the wire. See that your thumb is close to the plier's jaw as much as possible to get a sharp bend.

Making an eye loop

Eye loops are made for projects where P-shaped loops won't do the needed job.

1. Begin by cutting out about three inches of a wire string.
2. Use bent chain-nose pliers to turn the wire through a right angle, i.e., 90°. This angle must be about ½" or ¾" away from one of the ends of the wire string.
3. Use round-nose pliers to hold the short end of the wire string. Ensure that the mouth is placed as close to the mouth as possible.
4. Use one hand to hold the round-nose pliers and then, the thumb of the other hand to tug the wire string up and across the jaws of the round-nose pliers. After doing this procedure, the string will look like a U-shape that is turned upside down.

5. Hold the wire in the jaws of the plier again to turn this U-shaped loop into an eye loop. Then, direct the wire strings within the jaws of the pliers so that the tool and the strings are now pointing horizontally.

6. Pull the wire string out of the jaw of the pliers so that you can cut the excesses with your flush cutter. Place the edge of the cutting tool at the point where the tail passes the stem. The flat side of the tool should be the one next to the side with the loop.

7. Once you cut the excess string, the loop will be open a bit. To close the loop, use a bent chain-nose plier to twist the wire's mouth.

Chapter 5

Wire Wrapping Project Ideas

Wire-Wrapped Rings

Tools and Materials

- Pliers with a round nose.
- Pliers with a chain nose.
- Flush cutter.
- Ring Mandrel.
- 20 gauge craft wire (You can get about 1 to 1½ feet of wire per ring.)
- 10mm disc beads.
- 6 – 10mm round beads.
- Bead caps.

Procedures

1. Wrap a string of wire about a ring mandrel about two times. See that you leave a tag on the string

that is bigger than the internal dimensions your ring will be in.

2. Flip the mandrel over to its other side so that you can see the side that bears the grooves. Then, pass both ends of the wire through the central hole of the disc-shaped bead. The bead should already have an opening. Then, tug the sides of the bead so that it sits at the base where the two sure ends meet. If you are using a glass bead for your project, make sure you don't rug it down too harshly as that can lead to it breaking.

3. Now, tug down a bead cap over the first bead that you worked with in step 2, while following that line of string.

4. You would notice that the two ends of the wire string have formed a straight mouth. Now, you will tug each end in a direction opposite the other, i.e., one should go towards the left and the other, towards the right.

5. Now, you can push the ring off the mandrel. You have to go through this process as gently as possible. When it is off, you would notice that the strings have formed a circular shape.

6. Twist one end of the metal string about the ring's base. Do this procedure about five times or to a point where there's nothing left of the string.

7. In case the wire string is too long, you can cut off the excess with a flush cutter while ensuring that the blade's flat side is the one that stays proximal to the end of the excess wire. Here, you are looking to get a smooth edge that does not protrude out of the ring's circles.

8. For the other end of the wire, repeat the procedures above from step 4.

9. You are done!

Let's look at a different way you can get this kind of ring done again. You could try adding a swirl design to the center top of the ring. To do that, follow the procedures below.

1. Twist the wire string about the ring mandrel two times before passing the final edge through the opening of a disc bead.

2. Pull out the ring from the mandrel's frame.
3. Along with your thumb and the tips of your other fingers, use round-nosed pliers to twist the two ends of the wire string about the tool's mouth. With the tool, make a swirl shape. The strings you use shouldn't be too stiff so that you can easily get them twirled.

4. After getting the base twirl, you can stop using the pliers and then, work with your fingers for

the rest of the circular twirls that will sit at the top of the bead.

5. Take one end of the wire string and twirl it about the edge closest to the bead. Use this technique to twirl the other end of the wire string.

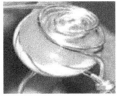

6. Use the flush cutter tool to cut of the rest wire that cannot fit the circular ring. For this project, you need not focus too much on getting too concentric whorls of string. The irregularity is what makes it beautiful.
7. You are done!

Fibula Pin

Tools and Materials

- Pliers with a round nose.
- Pliers with a chain nose.
- A flush cutter.
- A bench block.
- A chasing hammer.
- A jeweler's file.
- 10mm beads
- Charms (not compulsory)
- Grade two emery paper.
- Copper wire string of gauge number 18 and a length of 4 inches.
- Craft wire of gauge number 24 and a length of 6 inches.

Procedures

1. Use a round-nose plier to round the end of an 18-gauge wire string into a small circle.

2. While gripping that wired circle with the round-nose plier, turn the rest length of the wire about with your thumb and forefinger. Turn the string in a circular pattern, creating neat swirls in the process. In this project, you need a wire that can be easily twirled, so you can go for a copper wire.

3. You can twist the wire in the opposite direction to create a wavy kind of style. You can go ahead swirling the wire to any style you want.

4. When you are done adding twirls and wavy effects to the wire string, use the round nose pliers to create a hook that heads toward your direction. You can close the pin by gripping the hook over the top.

5. You can fuse the end of the wire with the loop with a chain-nose plier.

6. Twist the wire below the loop (about ½ inches below.) With this design, the loop of the ring is parallel to the direction of the swirls of the string.

7. Get the 24-gauge sure and then, twist it about the bottom of the hooked part of the string. To twist the string, use your thumb and forefingers while making sure to exact only a little pressure. If you

feel the grip of the swirls is not tight enough, you could work with your chain-nose pliers.

8. Next, twist the craft wire string along the straight end in a neat design.

9. You can use a flush cutter to cut off the excess part of the wire string while seeing that the tool's sharp edge is the one that sits closest to the piece. This technique will help you to make clean cuts and to prevent your skin from getting ripped by any sharp edge the ring has.

10. Place your project on the bench block and then, hit it gently with a chasing hammer to make it flat and compact.

11. To get a smooth finish, work with the hammer's flat edge. For a rougher finish, work with the round edge of the hammer. Repeat this technique after flipping the project over.

12. You can choose several kinds of beads that you can add to the pin. Thread the beads through the straight end of the wire project.
13. You are done!

Barrette

Tools and Materials

- Pliers with a round nose.
- Pliers with a chain nose.
- Flush cutter.
- 1 yard of a 24-gauge craft wire.
- 1 large-sized barrette.
- Mother disc beads of about 10mm.
- Crystal or water-pearl beads (4mm, 6mm, and 8mm.)

Procedures

1. You would see several holes in a barrette. Thread one end of the wire string through one of the holes.

2. Wrap one of the edges of the wire about the barrette hole you are working with. Once you are sure that the wrap is tight enough, you can cut the excesses of the wire string behind the barrette. After, push the cut end under the barrette.

3. Thread one mother disc bead to the center top of the barrette. To keep it in place, wrap the wire tightly around the base.

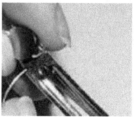

4. You can continue passing the wire through the wrapped end to keep it in place. Afterward, continue with a second flat bead. See that you are not wrapping the wire string around the barrette's bent spring.

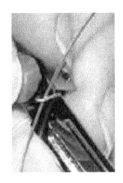

5. You can go on with securing the beads across the whole length of the barrette by rolling the string around the whole base. You could also pass the string through the holes in the metal. Just see that you are fastening each roll of wire as you thread the beads through the string.

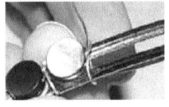

6. You can tighten the wrapped wire with chain-nose pliers. You would notice that the crystal beads have tinier openings in comparison to the rest. This is because of its small size. So, to get this bead threaded, make use of a

narrower string of wire. An example of a narrow wire string is the 24-gauge wire.

7. As you thread the beads, you'd eventually get to the end of the barrette. There, thread the wire through the hole that sits at the top. Once the crystal beads have filled the span of the barrette, you can surround them with smaller beads with diameters of 4mm, 8mm, and 6mm. For ornate purposes, use shiny beads.

8. Pass the wire back through the top of the barrette. You can use a few beads to hold the wire in place by twisting the wire around the back, and end of the barrette. To give your barrette an added height, you could allow an inch of wire string to come out at its end.

9. You can go on adding beads to the wire string while ensuring that you twist it regularly. This technique will help you secure the beads until you get to the end of the barrette. If you are satisfied with the number of beads spanning the barrette's length, you could stop here. If you still aren't satisfied, you could turn the wire string the other way and then, begin to thread the beads through it.

10. Pass the wire through the hole at the end of the barrette to keep the string of beads in place.

11. You can twist the wire about the barrette's bottom before going ahead to cut off the excess string with a flush cutter. To end this process, keep the end of the string buried in the knot.

12. The beads you choose to work with as well as the style with which you twist the wires will determine the class of barrettes you make.

Swarovski Crystal Cluster Earrings

Tools and Materials

- Pliers with a round nose.
- Pliers with a chain nose.
- Flush cutter.
- Two French hooks.
- Twenty-eight headpins.
- Jump rings.
- Thirty-two Swarovski crystals (different colors.) You could get 2 double-coned crystals with a diameter of 8mm, 24 double-coned crystals of 6mm, and lastly, 6 double-coned crystals of 4mm diameter.

Procedures

1. String a crystal with a diameter of 8mm to the top of a headpin.

2. Cut the headpin a few centimeters away from the bead. An easier way to follow through with this technique is to bend the pin a few centimeters from the bead before cutting it. This way, you can be sure of the distance before cutting.

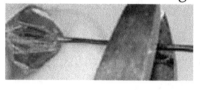

3. Use round-nose pliers to form a loop at the top of the headpin. Then, you can tighten the loop at the top by squeezing the handles of the pliers together. See that the final loop is flush against the bead.

4. Repeat these procedures from step 2 on thirty-one different hairpins, while moving from the biggest hairpin to the smallest. Make sure each crystal earring is held back with a loop. Divide the crystals into two sections, with each running to sixteen.

5. While holding the jump ring with the tips of your forefingers, use your chain-nose pliers to twist it open. See that you don't push the ring on both ends to avoid putting too much pressure on it.

6. Hold down one end of the jump ring with chain-nose pliers. After, fix a large crystal to the ring before going ahead to add a small crystal. See that the large crystal sits below the small crystal.

7. You can string more beads to the jump ring. Here is the stage where you make your own arrangements and designs. All you need to ensure is that you do not string two different colors of beads together on the jump ring. Try to use different sizes of beads too. Lastly, alternate the number of beads per ring. Note that the beads talked about here are the looped hairpins.

8. Once you have up to three looped beads on a jump ring, see that the smallest one is located towards the outer edge.

9. If you want a thick and wide piece, add as many looped beads as possible to the jump ring.

10. To close the jump ring, twist the ends together with the tips of your fingers. As you work, use the mouth of the pliers to grip the other end.

11. Make another jump ring loaded with looped beads. After, join the two bunches of jump rings. This technique will give your earrings the dangling effect.

12. You can keep on adding several loaded jump rings until you attain the length of earring you desire. You could also stop after you have finished using all the looped beads.

13. The next thing to do is work with a French hook. First, turn the ball up before twisting the loop open. Just follow the same technique you used for the jump rings. However, you should not bend a French hook too much as it is relatively fragile.

14. Fix the dangling bunch of jump rings to the French hook so that the crystal with the eight-millimeter diameter stays at the bottom of the string. After loading the hook, close up the French hook before allowing the ball to go back to rest.

15. To make the earring for the other ear, repeat the procedures above, from step 5 to step 14.
16. You are done.

Wire Loop Earrings

Tools and Materials

- Pliers with a round nose.
- Pliers with a chain nose.
- Flush cutter.
- A 22 gauge craft wire with strips of two eight-inch strings and two 3-inch strings.
- 68 drop beads with an opening at their mouths.
- Two round beads (8mm or 9mm inch diameter.)

- 2 beads that you can suspend from the central portion of round, oval, and heart-shaped loops. You could work with any shape though.
- 2 French hooks.

Procedures

1. Create a loop with your round-nose pliers, going an inch from each end of the eight inches long wire strip.
2. Twist the wire's short end two or three times around the loop's base.
3. Cut off the excess of the string with your flush cutter. After this, you can leave your beads spread out and ready for your project.
4. On a wire string, thread about seventeen of the drop beads.

5. Add a bigger bead to the string. It is this bead that would be at the central part of the loop.

6. After the big bead, add seventeen more drop beads to the wire string.
7. Use round-nose pliers to pass the wire's open end into the loop. This joint should be a few inches from the point where the beads end.

8. Grip the loop with chain-nose pliers. After, wrap the wire string about the base twice or thrice.

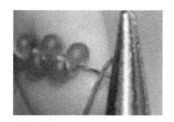

9. Get rid of the excess string with a flush cutter. Make sure you cut the string very close to its base.

10. Use your chain-nose pliers to cut through the wire string so that the edges you trimmed previously does not come out of the knot. At this stage, your beads should not be packed too tightly together. You will know the reason for this technique in the step below.

11. Now, use your fingers to bend the wire into an arc. If you made the beads too tightly packed together, the string could snap into two at this

stage because of the increased pressure on the string.

12. Grab the 3-inch wire and then, form a loop at the tip with round-nose pliers.
13. Grip the loop with chain-nose pliers before twirling the wire string around with your thumb and forefinger. Just twirl the string into two loops.

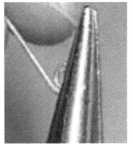

14. String the bead you want to fix at the earring's center at this stage.

15. Make a loop with the wire string by fixing the round-nose pliers a few inches above the top of the bead.

16. Grip the loop you formed above with chain-nose pliers before wrapping the bottom of the string about three times. This technique will help hold the bead in place.

17. You can go on to cut off the excess wire string with a flush cutter. Then, turn the sharp edge of the string towards the inner whorl.

18. Use your thumb, forefinger, and chain-nose pliers to pull a jump-ring open by twisting the two ends apart.

19. Fix one side of the loop to the jump ring.

20. You can fix a central dangle bead to the major project if you like.
21. Add the other end of the loop to the jump ring.

22. To close the jump ring, twist the ends tightly together.
23. Grab the French hook, and then, push up the ball that lies over the loop's base. Then, pull open the loop by twisting it around. After that, fix the loop of the beads to it.

24. Close the French hook by twisting the ends around with your round nose pliers.
25. To make the second earring, repeat the procedures from the first step.

26. You are done!

Cabochon Penchant

Tools and Materials

- Pliers with a round-nose.
- Pliers with chain-nose.
- Flush cutter.
- Vise
- Wire twister
- Alligator clips.
- 40 × 30 oval-shaped cabochon.
- 20-gauge of silver craft wire. Get two of these strings with each a length of 1 foot.
- Three feet of 24-gauge silver craft wire.

- 1 foot of 24-gauge of copper wire.
- A chain to fix your pendant.
- Small beads.

Procedures

1. Cut out a foot of the 24-gauge silver wire. After, hold down the 24-gauge copper and the silver wire in a vise-tight grip. You can then set the rest of the silver wire for use at a later date.
2. Clamp the wires at the opposite end with a wire twister. Ensure that the wire strings are held down securely before locking down the clamp.

3. You can use one hand to tug on the back lever of the wire twister. While doing that, leave the handles to roll in a circle through your other hand. (Your other hand should be clenched in a loose grip.) You can manage the degree of

looseness or tightness you twist the wire strings through. If the wire was twisted too tightly, you will know at once. To save yourself this stress, you could just purchase an already twisted wire. However, you could twist some of the wires yourself as it will help you become even more creative. Besides, you would be able to merge two different colors of wire—copper and silver—which is a chance that most pre-twisted strings are in.

4. Once the wires are twisted tightly enough, project them out of the vise. Make sure the wire is wrapped so tightly that it doesn't loosen shortly after.
5. Arrange the twisted wire string in between the two 20-gauge wire strings.

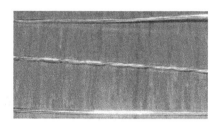

6. See that the twisted wire string sits in the middle. Afterward, grip the ends of the three strings with alligator clips. Ensure that the wires are a few inches away from each other and that the tips are well secured in the teeth of the clip.

7. Cut out a 4-inch piece of 24-gauge silver craft wire before you wrap it about the center of the rest wire strings. Make sure the strings are kept in order with the twisted wires in the middle. To keep the wires flat as you wrap, work with your pliers.

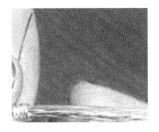

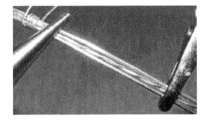

8. Continue coiling a single string of wire about the three groups of wires. Do this procedure eight times.

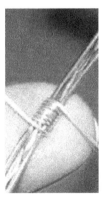

9. When you are done coiling the single wire string, cut the edge of the wire flush with a flush cutter.

See that the edge faces the cabochon's surface so it does not appear on the finished piece.

10. You can cut another 4-inch piece of a 24-gauge silver wire. Coil the single wire strand you used earlier to the left side of the first coil. Do this procedure about eight times. After, cut the wire inside to keep the end of the wire out of sight.

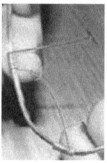

11. Bend the wire around the cabochon while keeping the wires arranged in a stack. Move the clip up to allow for more wire strings to move around the stone.

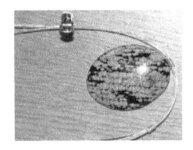

12. Remove the clip from the other end of the joint strings before twisting a 4-inch piece of wire about them. Do this process towards the right sure of the coil. As you work, make sure that the wires at kept flat and stacked so that they appear neat when you fix them to the stone.

13. Once you bend the wire around the cabochon, the two twisted ends will dangle at the midpoint of either side. If you don't make the joint too tight, you can either move the strings upwards or downwards until you get them centered.

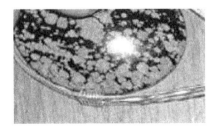

14. While the joint wires are kept about the stone, begin to push one of its ends in an L-shape at the top. This point is where you make the bail.

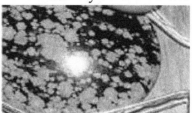

15. Grab the wire piece after setting the cabochon in one direction. From there, take the wire from one side and then, twist it at the point where you made the creases. Here, all you need to do is wrap the five wire strings once or twice around the creases tightly enough to keep the strings compact.

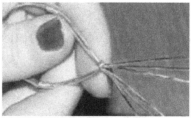

16. Fix the cabochon back at the center of the stack of wire strings. You would notice that the cabochon fits just tightly into the confines. As you push the cabochon in, tug the bottom wire towards the

center of the back. Repeat this process with the front of the cabochon.

17. Here, pull down the wire strings for the curlicues that will embellish the cabochon's face. Then, tug the three wires downwards towards the face at the front. Include the twisted wire string here. See that the bail is big enough that it can be fixed to a chain too.

18. Hold down each strand of the rest wire strands with round-nose pliers. Each should be about ½ inches above the top of the cabochon.

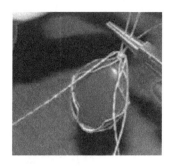

19. Turn one of the wires down in a direction that is towards the back of the cabochon. After, create a notch at the base of the cabochon so that you can wrap the bail around it.

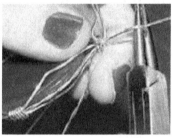

20. Do the above procedure for the other wire. This technique will help you create the same notch for the other side of the bail.

21. While working with the same wire that you used to wrap about the wire strands, pass the wire around the back of the cabochon to catch the notch you just made.

22. Wrap the wire string as many times as possible. This step is what makes your project beautiful.

23. Cut out the excess wire strings that hang down the bail with a flush cutting tool. Cut the string very close to the base. If you have another wire string coming out, bend it inside so that you can bend it within the joint wire strings. This technique will prevent the sharp edges from catching on any rough surface.

24. Assemble the beads you want to use for the curlicues.

25. Cut out the rest of the three wires so that they don't hang down the stone.

26. Thread some beads onto the twisted wire strings. The number of beads you thread on the string depends on the style you are working with.

27. To keep the beads in place, wrap the twisted wire strings around with your round-nose pliers. Make a small loop at the end.

28. Grip the loop you made with your chain-nose pliers before using your fingers to twist the ends into a swirl.

29. Use round-nose pliers to make a corkscrew with the other twisted wire. Add beads to the rest of the wire's length before securing it to the wire string that keeps the cabochon in place.

30. You can either coil or bead the third wire strand. When you are done, tuck the third strand into the bottom of the wire with chain-nose pliers.

31. After you have done the beading or coiling, use the chain-nose pliers to twist the wires at the back of the cabochon. Bend the wires at their centers to hold them in place. Repeat this procedure at the front of the cabochon too. Here, the third craft wire was twirled at the front.

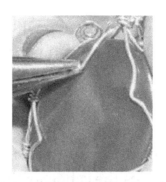

32. You are done!

Triple Strand Cluster Necklace

Tools and Materials

- Pliers with a round nose.
- Pliers with a chain nose.
- Flush cutter.
- Bench block.
- Chasing hammer
- Crimping tool for crimp beads.
- Crimp beads (size 2.)
- Delicas (size 11)
- Crimp covers.
- 1 foot of 16-gauge wire.
- Twenty-eight spacers (6mm)
- Nine spacers (9 or 10mm)
- Cube beads (4 × 4 mm)
- 36 Czech crystal beads.
- 36 Swarovski crystals (4 mm diameter.)

Procedures guiding the making of a necklace with a wiry swirl

1. Use round-nose pliers to make a loop at one end of the craft wire.

2. Use your thumb, forefinger, and chain-nose pliers to roll about half of the wire string into a tight spiral.

3. Do the above procedure at either end of the wire. However, for this side, twist the string in the opposite direction. Once this process is completed, you'd see something in the shape of an S.

4. Use a chasing hammer to hit the spiral wire string while it is on a bench block. To get a nice finish, use the flat edge of the hammer. For something more defined and rough, use the round edge. When you are finished with one end, flip it over and continue with the next.

Now, you can use this spiral creation to make different things. The first five steps listed above here are starting steps of some sort. We will also be employing the use of crimp covers in this project. They are used to cover crimp beads as they give the project a new look.

Necklaces.

1. First, you would need to bring together their pieces of wire string. After, thread the wire strings through the bead's opening.

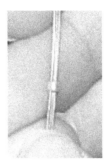

2. Now, pass the joined wire strings through the spiral ring that is located very close to the exterior.

3. Here, you will bend the three strings in the opposite direction so that you can thread them again through the crimp bead. This way, the strings would get a ribbon kind of look.

4. To create a U-shaped crimp bead, press down on it with the back notch of a crimping tool. Afterward, move the tool through a quarter circle, as if you want to form a crescent-shape.

While you are still with the crimping tool, grip the crimp bead with its front notch. Then, press down on the bead with the tool again to create the shape of a ball.

5. Now, you can cover the bead with a crimp cover.

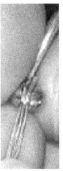

6. Use chain-nose pliers to keep the bead closed and tightened.

7. Now, moving on to the wire strands, thread three delicas through it. Afterward, thread in one Swarovski crystal, then, add three more delicas. See that the ends of the wire strings are threaded through the strands with beads. The crystals and beads usually have holes big enough to size two threading of wire strings.

8. Thread one strand of wire string through the beads before trimming the remaining strand with a flush cutter.

9. Thread 3 delicas, one Czech crystal, and three more delicas on the second wire string. Now, pass the thread through the beads that were first threaded. Now, trim the short edges again with the flush cutter.

10. Thread one delica, one cube, one delica, one cube, and lastly one delica (You could follow whichever pattern you desire.) Once you are done, pass the end through the beads. Trim the remaining with a flush cutter.

11. Now that you have threaded the strings through the beads and trimmed the excesses, you can now bead it into a necklace.

12. Feed a small spacer through the three strands of wire strings.

13. Place the spacer close to the cluster of beads. This necklace requires about eight groups of four cluster beads and two groups of the two cluster beads. If you work with this technique, you will get a 14-inch necklace. Ensure that the necklace is long enough to go over your neck as there's no clasp for it.

14. If you want to make another bead cluster, ensure that you follow the same sequence as the first one.
15. Thread a big spacer onto the wire string.
16. Ensure that the spacer is tightly pressed to the rest of the beads.

17. You can continue making beaded clusters as it will only increase the length of the necklace. However, you should only fix the large spacer to it after the fourth cluster of beads.

18. As you go on adding the beaded clusters, see that they are pulled closer together.

19. It'd be great if the necklace were symmetrical, i.e., with equal numbers of beaded clusters on each side. After that, string the three wire strings of the other end through a crimp bead.

20. Pass the three strings through the outermost curve of the metal swirl we made at first.

21. Feed the wire strings back through the crimp bead so that you get a loop knot.

22. Tuck each of the three wire strings through three beads.
23. To see that the wire strings are straight out of the bead, tug lightly at it.

24. Use the crimping tool to tighten the crimp bead.
25. You can cut off the excess strings with your flush cutter.
26. Fix the crimp cover over the crimp bead.
27. Tighten the crimp cover with the chain-nose pliers.

28. You are done! While making this necklace though, you could make use of several colors of beads to make it more ornate. And remember that it has to be long enough to go about your neck.

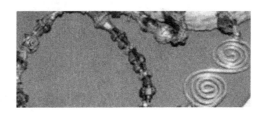

Twist-and-Wrap Bracelet

Tools and Materials

- Round-nose pliers.
- Chain-nose pliers.
- Flush cutter.
- Bench block.
- Chasing hammer.
- 3 different 22-gauge wires. For each, see that it is about 1½ feet long.
- 6 inches of 16-gauge wire.

- 15 beads of different colors and shapes.
- 100 beads—seed beads, cubical beads, round beads, etc.
- Silver and golden beads.

Procedures

1. Thread a big bead two inches away from the end of a 22-gauge wire.

2. Tie a simple knot above the big bead with the wire string to keep it in place.

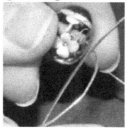

3. Add more big beads, all the while, tying knots above them to hold them in place. As you string the beads together, see that you keep them apart

from each other with a distance of 1inch. You can string about six beads this way. The bracelet must be long enough to go round your wrist.

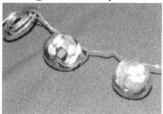

4. As you string the beads together, leave about a two inches long wire string at their ends.

5. You can start to form a hook for this bracelet now. Here, we will be working with an S-shaped hook. To start, bend one end of the 16-gauge wire into a small circle with a round-nose plier.

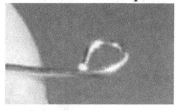

6. Use your chain-nose pliers to add more twirls to the hook.

7. Once you twist the wire string close to its central point, grip the twirled part with your round-nose pliers. Then, start to bend the wire in a direction

that is away from your body. Bend the wire into something that looks like a pelican.

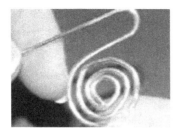

8. Use the flat side of the flush cutter to grip the wire string, while ensuring that there are about 1½ inches left.
9. Roll the end of the remaining wire string into a small circle with round-nose pliers.

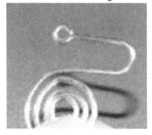

10. After curving the loop at the top of the wire twirl, you can now start to beat it into a flat shape.
11. Here, you will work with a chasing hammer. Use the flat edge of the hammer to beat the string twirls. You could beat either side of the twirls so that the wire doesn't become too weak.

12. Pass the S-shaped hook through the end of the baseline wire string before forming a loop. Grip this loop with chain-nose pliers. Then, use your fingers to roll the wire string about the baseline so that it is kept in place. Roll the wire about three times.

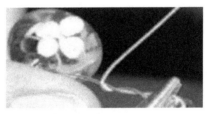

13. Tighten the wire you wrapped before cutting off the excesses.

14. Make another loop at the other end of the wire string. Since we are not making a clasp for this bracelet, this loop is the part that the other part of the hook will cling unto. Now, use beads to fill the gap between the large beads at the base. See

that the beads you use here are smaller and are of different colors.

15. You can roll another length of a 22-gauge wire beneath the first bead so that it keeps it in place. After, thread a medium-sized bead and a few chips of bead through the wire. This technique is to use the beads to fill the gap that exists between the large beads.

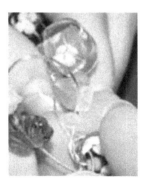

16. Bend the wire string into an arc before wrapping it beneath the second bead on the baseline. Keep it in place by tying a knot under it too. The reason

this arc has to be there is to get beads that can move freely about the length of the wire string.

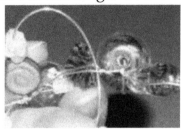

17. Repeat the above procedure as you move across the length of the bracelet. The density of your bracelet depends on the shape of beads you use, the kind of beads you start with, and the ones you use to fill the gaps between the big beads. For this bracelet, you wouldn't want to see too much space in between the large beads.

18. Grip the wire string at one side of any of the floating beads with a chain-nose plier. Then, twist the wire string in a clockwise direction so that the bead is kept in place. Follow the same technique at the bead's other end if it can still move about freely. Repeat the two techniques for the other floating beads.

19. Now, the bracelet should have three beaded wire strings, with each bead held tightly in place by the wire twists.

20. If there is an excess of wire string, you can thread it through the bracelet again in the opposite direction. If you don't have an excess, you can start a new wire string. For this additional length, thread in small beads. It is the small bead that gives the bracelet a finished look.

21. To keep the wire string in place, feed a new bead through the wire string. Then, weave the wire through the bead's hole. One thing you need to be careful of here is the kind of outer coating your bead has. For example, faux pearls can easily get scratched, so, you need to be careful.

22. As you feed the wire strings with beads, find the empty parts of the bracelet, i.e., the part with no beads, then, fill it with small beads. To avoid a strain across the bracelet, see that you twist the wire strings in the same direction. Also, to

prevent a heavy piece, thread the beads evenly on the string at either end.

23. Twist the excess wire string at the base of the bracelet at either end to keep the wire that was threaded through the beads in place. You should not bother about the density of wires as they only help to keep your bracelet compact and sturdy.

24. Twisting the wire strings will increase the strength of the bracelet. Also, if you thread the wire strings through the beads about three times, you would be able to eradicate the susceptibility of it breaking. Your bracelet should also have a prominent top and a bottom.

25. When you are done filling and twisting, curve the bracelet so that the two hooks meet, i.e., the loop at one end intertwines with the twirled sure strings at the other end.

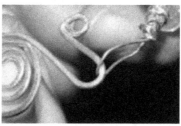

26. You are done!

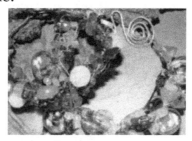

Coil Bracelet

Tools and Materials

- Round nose pliers.
- Chain nose pliers.
- Flush cutter.
- Coiling Gizmo

- Bench block.
- Chasing hammer.
- 1 yard of a 22-gauge copper wire.
- 15-inch length of an 18-gauge craft wire.
- 15-inch length of a 14-gauge craft wire.
- Beads with diameters ranging from 6 to 15 inches.
- Metal rings.

Procedures

1. Start by twisting one end of the copper wire around the loop of the coil in Gizmo. This twist will help support the wire string.

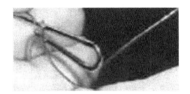

2. Roll the wire string three times about the Gizmo coil.
3. Ensure that the wire dangles from the loop so that you can attach the coiling Gizmo.

4. Hold the wire's long end to the bracket's flat side with your thumb. Then, start to twist the loop's handle to form the coils. To get a neat outline, wrap the copper wire evenly while going one layer at a time.

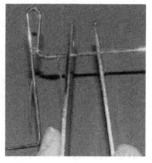

5. After wrapping the copper wire fully, free the coil by trimming the wire that is wrapped about the anchor loop.

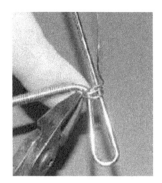

6. Now, drag the coiled copper wire off the Gizmo coil and then, cut off the excess length.
7. Thread the 18-gauge wire through the coil. See that the craft wire's length is three times that of the coil.
8. Now, wrap the craft wire about the coiling Gizmo.

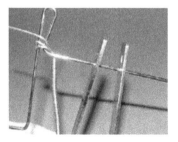

9. To twist this wire string, turn the handle of the coiling Gizmo.

10. This technique we employed here will fetch us another coil, but it will be a much thinner one. Coil the wire to a length that just slightly exceeds that of the copper wire. Then, cut off the excess strings. When you are done, drag this could off the Gizmo too before beginning another one.

11. To make a plain coil, just go ahead to twist the wire about the Gizmo before it is threaded through the craft wire.

12. Cut an 8-inch length of the 14-gauge craft wire. After, curve one end into a loop that is shaped like a teardrop. The loop has to be wide enough so that the bracelet's clasp can fit through it at the end.

13. After, roll 6-inches of the 22-gauge copper wire around the base of the loop. Do this neatly so that you can have neat rings between the loop and the bracelet.

14. This is the stage where you feed the coils and the beads through the craft wire. Here, you can follow any sequence of your choice.

15. For the thin coils, feed in the bigger beads.

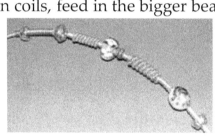

16. After feeding in all the beads, use the round-nose pliers to form a loop at the end you at still working on. However, see that there's still a portion of the wire that the wire can wrap about.

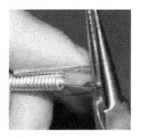

17. Trim the excess of the wire string with a flush cutting tool.

18. Roll 6-inches of the 22-gauge wire around the loop's neck. You can start this wrapping at the bottom of the loop and then, move upwards.

19. The moment the wire wraps about the bottom of the loop completely, you would notice a gradual slope. Trim the excess wire strings with your flush cutter before tucking the sharp ends within the loop.

20. Curve the wire into the shape of a bangle. Do not let the two ends meet as you curve.

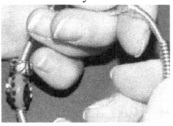

21. Flatten one end of the rest of the 14-gauge wire string with a chasing hammer. After hammering one side, move over to the other side.

22. You can create a small loop at the string's flat end with round-nosed pliers.

23. Curve the wire at a distance of ½ inch away from the loop. After, you can think of the size you want the clasp to assume. To keep the loop small, cut a portion of the wire string so that the twirled part is in place.

24. Still on the 14-gauge wire string, to create a small loop in the opposite direction. Start by twirling the wire string into spirals.

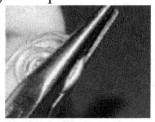

25. Use your thumb and chain-nose pliers to finish the spirals. Here, since we at working with a tougher sure string, you might need to add more pressure to the plier's handles.

26. Once you get to the coil's outer edge, see that the gap that exists between the coils is wide enough for the clasp to fit into.

27. Hit the twirled clasp with the chasing hammer to make it flat. Do the hammering against a bench block. While hammering, know that the

hammer's flat edge leaves the project with a smooth finish. The round edge leaves the project looking rough. You can flip the clasp over to continue hammering it.

28. Push the clasp through the loop.

29. After, tighten the spiral at a point ahead of the loop to keep it secure and in place.
30. Clasp the ends together to finish making your bracelet.

Knitted Bracelets

Tools and Materials

- Knitting tube and needle.
- Two alligator clips.
- A heavy stone (or any 1 pound weight).
- Chain-nose pliers.
- Flush cutter.
- A crimping tool for size 2 crimp beads.
- Tiger tail wire.
- Seed bead mix.
- 2 bead cones.
- 2 stones.
- 2 silver balls.
- Oval stone of dimension 15 by 20 mm.
- 2 crimp beads and their covers.

Procedures

1. Fix an alligator clip to one of the ends of the thread. This way, the clip can prevent the beads from falling out of the string as you assemble the piece. You can then proceed to feed the beads past 1½ inches of the string.

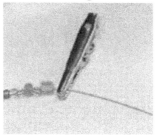

2. Pass the other end of the thread through the uppermost edge of the knitting tube.

3. Use an alligator clip to fix the weight (stone) to the end of the thread you just passed through the knitting tube. To avoid kinks along the thread, keep it straight as you thread it through the tube.

4. Start to wrap the thread around a peg. Start at the farthest peg and then, continue in an anticlockwise direction. Move over to wound the thread about the outer peg.

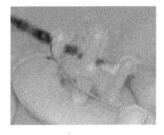

5. Use the technique above to connect the thread through all the pegs. Start from the outer path and then, slowly head to the inner paths. See that

you keep on moving in a counterclockwise direction.

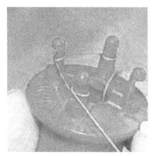

6. Once you wrap the thread around the four pegs, fix your needle to the last strand of the thread. As you do so, place your finger at the top of the peg so that the threads don't come off them.

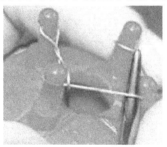

7. Lift the last thread over the top of the peg. After that, take the needle away. Even with this technique, one loop must remain on the peg.

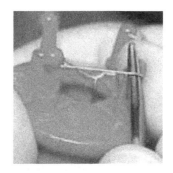

8. Do the procedures listed above for the rest of the pegs. If you don't want the strings to leave the pegs, see that you regularly push them down.

9. As you go forward, use your hand to hold down the thread wound about the pegs.

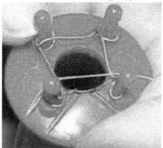

10. Now, you can tug the strung beads that we made at first towards the end of the string. After that, use the clip again to prevent the beads from falling out of the wire string

11. Thread two beads to the top of the thread and then, make it straight so that they fall in between the pegs on the knitting tool. Afterward, wrap the wire around the pegs to the right side of the previous one.

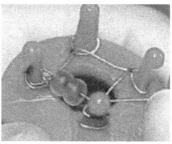

12. Raise the loop at the bottom over the peg that now bears the beads thread.

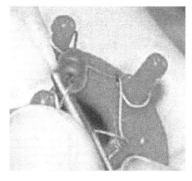

13. Ensure that one loop still sits on the peg.

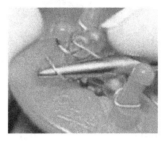

14. Add two or three beads in between each stitch. If you want, you can thread in bigger beads. Just ensure that the thread remains at the base of the pegs as you continue.

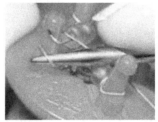

15. As you continue, pull the bracelet's middle so that it can be fed through the knitting tube's center.

16. To continue, add about three beads, and then, loop the thread around the pegs that are above the beads. Then, use the bottom edge of the thread below the beads to form a loop around the peg. Don't forget to pull at the middle of the beaded string through the center of the tube.

17. To finish, pass the mouth of the thread through the two strings of thread sitting across each peg.

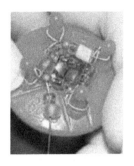

18. Now, remove the thread from the knitting tube completely. You could use your needle to loosen the threads from their pegs by lifting the narrow strings.

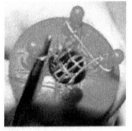

19. Form a loop with the mouth of the thread through a nearby knitted section. To tighten the knot, pull at that free end firmly. As you continue, push the knot to the bottom of the knitted part. Ensure that the knot you make here is tight enough.

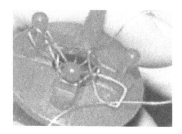

20. Pull the bracelet out of the knitting tube, and then, feed a bead cone through one of the ends so that the knot is protected.

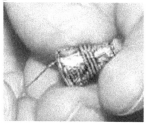

21. Now, string a small stone, a silver ball, a crimp head, and then, a large stone.

22. Finish the other end with stones arranged in a beautiful sequence. You can embellish this

sequence so much that the thread is filled enough to make a diameter of about 7½ inches.

23. Pass the thread through the large bead and then, the crimp bead should be on the opposite side of the bracelet. Repeat this technique with the other end of the bracelet. This way, you will end up with the thread fed through the beads twice.

24. To get the two ends of the bracelet together, tug at the thread to tighten it. Work with a crimping tool to tighten the crimp beads. After that, fix the crimp covers to it.

25. Cut off the excess string with the flush cutting tool. Be careful as you cut off the excesses so that the other parts of the thread are protected.
26. You are done!

Eye Pin Pendant Bail

Tools and Materials

- Chain-nose pliers.
- Rosary pliers with a side cutter.
- ¾″ of title bead.
- Natural Brass eye pin, 1½ inches.

Procedures

1. Curve the eye pin into a U-shape. See that the loop you make with the pin is about ¼ inches

above the bead. The pendant side does not have looped ends and they should be ½ inches above the beaded pendant.

2. Coil the end of the pin that is not curved into a loop around the end that is looped. After, tighten the loop with the chain-nose pliers. After this procedure, your penchant is ready.

3. To feed the bead into the eye pin, grip the turtle bead by the side. Then, push the eye pin back through the bead's hole.

4. You are done.

Wig Jig Bracelet

Tools and Materials

- 12 Swarovski crystals with a diameter of 8mm.
- 4 metal round beads with a diameter of 2.5mm.
- 15 inches of a 16-gauge wire, 18-gauge wire, and 20-gauge wire.
- 30 inches of 20-gauge wire, 21-gauge wire, and 22-gauge wire.
- Clasp
- 3 inches of commercial chain for the guard chain.
- Flush cutter.
- Round-nose pliers.
- Bent Chain-nose pliers.
- Nylon-jaw pliers.
- Wig Jig Centaur.
- Step-jaw pliers.

Procedures

This project has several components. To make the first one for the 3-looped string, follow these guidelines;

1. Cut about 5¼ inches long of the 16, 18, and 20-gouge wire. You should use soft wire strings for this project as they are easy to bend.

2. Make a loop at one end of the wire string with round nose pliers or the step-jaw plier. Then, cut off the excesses with a flush cutter.

3. You can make the wire string straight by tugging them through the jaws of the nylon-jaw pliers.

4. Place the first and the second pegs in your jig. Then, fix the loop you made first on the first peg.

5. Wrap the wire string about the second peg tightly. Make sure you leave the wire string that is next to the empty hole for the third peg.

6. Taking care not to apply too much force on the wire string, wound it about the third peg so that it is next to the empty hole for the fourth peg.

7. Still, with little force, wrap the wire string about the fourth peg, but make sure that the string is next to the empty hole for the fifth peg.

8. Add one more peg, and lightly wound the wire string about it so that it is next to the empty hole for the sixth peg.

9. Wound the string about the sixth peg so that it is next to the empty hole for the seventh peg.

10. Wound the string about the seventh peg so that it is next to the empty hole for the eighth peg. Follow this technique for the eighth peg too.

11. Now, take the wire string from the jig and then, use the flush cutting tool to cut the excesses. Your flush cutter must be very close to the edge of the wire string.
12. Close the loop made on the eighth peg with bent chain-nose pliers.
13. Use your nylon-jaw pliers to press down on the wire part of the project. Do this procedure in several planes so that it is well flattened. After, you can bend the string with your fingers so that it is as symmetrical as possible.

To make the 2-loop component, follow these guidelines;

1. Cut out a part of the 16, 18, or 20-gauge wire. It has to be four inches long.
2. Create a loop at the end of this wire string with your round-nose pliers. The loop should be like a small circle.
3. You can make this string straight by moving it through the jaws of a nylon-jaw plier.
4. Fix the ninth and the tenth pegs in the jig before fixing the loop you made at first on the ninth peg.

5. Lightly wound the wire string through the tenth peg. Then, you can leave the wire that is next to the hole for the eleventh peg.
6. Add the eleventh peg to the project and then, wound the wire string around the twelfth leg so that it is next to the hole for the twelfth peg.
7. Add the twelfth peg to the project and again, lightly pass the wire string lightly about it so that is next to the hole for the thirteenth peg. Repeat this procedure for the 14th peg too.
8. Cut off the excesses of the wire string with the flush cutting tool. The flat side of this tool is to face the twists.
9. Use your chain-nose pliers to close the loop you made for the fourteenth peg.
10. Use your nylon-jaw pliers to press the wire part of the project. This technique will help keep the piece flat. You can finish your project by using your fingers to lightly bend the wire strings so that you can get something equal on both sides.
11. You can make two of these two-loop wire components.

The last component to make is the 2:1 wire component.

1. Cut out a part of the 16, 18, or 20-gauge wires. What you cut out should be about two inches long.
2. Create a small loop at the end of the wire string with round-nose pliers.
3. Make this wire string straight by tugging it out of the jaws of nylon-jaw pliers.
4. Fix the fifteenth and sixteenth pegs in the jig. Then, you can put the loop you made at first on the fifteenth peg.
5. Lightly wrap the wire string about the sixteenth peg so that it is next to the hole for the seventeenth peg.
6. Add the seventeenth peg and them, wrap the sure string about it.
7. You can now remove the wire from the jig after cutting out the wire excesses with a flush cutter.
8. Use your chain-nose pliers to close the loop you made for the seventeenth peg.
9. Use your nylon-jaw pliers to press the wiry component. This technique will make the string hard and flat. You can do the rest with your fingers to make it even on both sides.
10. See that you do two of these 2:1 wire components.

Now, the final stage involves threading the three components together.

1. We are going to begin this project from the central piece. First, construct a wrapped bead link to connect the uppermost loop on the 3-loop wire component to the 2-loop wire component. When threading these components together, use a wire string that will easily fit all the beads. For the bead link, use a 6mm bead and two 2.5mm bead.

2. When you are done with the first bead link, connect the left loop at the bottom of your 3-loop wire component to the right loop at the bottom of your 2-loop wire component.

3. Connect the 2-loop wire component to the adjacent side of the 3-loop wire component.

4. Now, connect the 2-loop wire component with the 2:1 wire component. Start by connecting the loops at the top with the bead link before going over to connect the loops at the bottom. Here, use one 6mm bead for the bead links.

5. Connect the right edge of the 2-loop component to the 2:1 wire component that is fixed to the right

side. For this step, work with two bead links. For the bead links here, use one of the 6mm beads.

6. You can complete the bracelet by using the two bead links to connect the single loop to the 2:1 wire to the clasp on either side. You can then add the bead links to either side before connecting the clasps. For the bead links, use the 6mm beads.

7. You are done!

Dangles

Tools and Materials

- 20, 22, 24-gauge round wire.
- Chain-nose pliers.
- Flush cutter.
- Round nose pliers.
- Crystal beads.

Procedures

1. Start with the 20, 22, or 24-gauge round wire. The wire string should be at least 3 inches long. For this project, it would be better if you used the biggest gouge of wire to thread your beads together.

2. Use your chain-nose pliers to grip the wire string a distance of 1 inch from its end. Then, turn the wire through a distance of ninety degrees.

3. Use the round-nose pliers to grip the one-inch gap that you left from the end of the wire. At the same time, see that the mouth of the round-nose poker is still close to the ninety-degree bend.

4. Use your thumb to push the wire over the jaw of the pliers. See that the string is very close to the pliers.

5. Place the wire string at a point that will help you finish a loop. Then, place the pliers horizontally to start making the loop.

6. To make a complete loop, push the wire string.

7. Before you remove the wire from the mouth of your pliers, set the end of the wire in a way that it is fixed on the loop's center. To finish this

procedure, you might need to tug the tail either towards the right or to the left till you get the central position.

8. Remove the wire from the mouth of the pliers and then, connect the loop you just made to the one you previously made in the project. The loop in question could be the one for the clasp or the one for the bead link.

9. Grip the half-completed loop with the chain-nose pliers. As you grip this segment, twist the short end around the longer end about two times.

10. Cut off the excess wire with a flush cutter.

11. To prevent the cut end from sticking out, you would need to squeeze and twist with chain-nose pliers.

12. Now, you can add few beads to the wire strings.

13. Push the beads down the string with the chain-nose pliers and then, instantly grip the wire string above the beads.

14. Turn the wire string through an angle of ninety degrees. The distance between the bead and the 90-degree bend determines the point where you will grip the wire string.

15. You can go on with the wrapped loop by passing the wire over the jaws of the pliers. Then, go through the procedures from the fourth step. After that, connect the two wire systems with the wrapped bead links.
16. You are done!

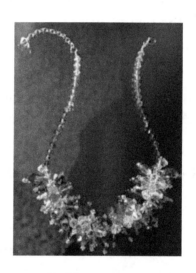

Ear Wire Finding

Tools and Materials

- Flush cutter.

- 20-gouge wire.
- Round-nose pliers.
- Chain-nose pliers.
- Beads of different colors.
- Nylon-jaw pliers.
- Pegs and jigs.
- Chasing hammer.

Procedures

1. Cut out three inches of the twenty-gouge round wire.
2. You can use nylon-jaw pliers to make this wire string flat.
3. Create an eye loop at one end of the wire string with round-nose pliers.
4. Push a 4mm bead down the wire. Ensure that it lies against the eye loop.
5. Grip the wire string at a point above the bead with a chain-nose plier. Then, use the mouth of the pliers to reduce the wire's thickness.
6. Turn the wire string through an angle of 80 degrees.

7. To turn the ear wire around a jig, use two metal pegs and a super reg. Use the first and second pegs to make the ear wires around the jig.
8. Now, twist the wire about the second peg so that it is next to the hole you made for the third peg. Do not apply too much force as you go through this process though.
9. Add one more peg and then, turn the wire against the third peg through an angle of thirty degrees.
10. Pull the ear wire from the jig and then, cut the wire ¼ inches from the bend at the third peg. Cut off the excesses with the flush cutter while heading towards the ear wire.
11. Use a nail file to smoothen the edges of the trimmed wire. You can also make the ends of the wire round with this same technique.
12. Use a chasing hammer to hit the rounded part of the ear wire. It is the rounded part of the wire that touches the Super reg. You can also use a nylon hammer to harden the rounded part of the ear wire without altering the wire's round shape.
13. This finished ear wire will match your earrings with similar beads tied to them.

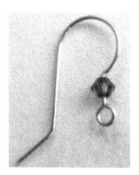

Confetti Earrings

Tools and Materials

- 6 lampwork beads (10mm to 15mm)
- 4 ivory freshwater pearls (4mm to 6mm)
- 4 pink freshwater pearls (4mm to 6mm)
- 4 light pink double coned crystals.
- 4 clear double coned crystals (4mm)
- 50 seed beads.
- 20-gauge sterling silver round wire.
- 24-gauge sterling silver round wire.
- 2 sterling silver ear wires.
- Round-nose pliers

- Chain-nose pliers.
- Flat-nose pliers.
- Wire cutters.
- Ruler.

Procedures

1. Cut out about 4½ inches in length of the 20-gauge wire string. This length will form the bottom of the earring. On one end of the wire, form a small loop with round-nose pliers. Using a small round-nose plier to do this part of the project will be better.
2. Now, use flat pliers to form a loop that is at a particular angle to the wire string.
3. While making sure that about 1½ inches of wire are left at one end of the wire, pass the rest of the string through the looped eye. It is this length that you will use to attach the string to the ear wire. You can also choose the shape you want to work with. There is the round shape and also, the teardrop shape. Well, in any case, either is good.
4. Make a small loop with the 1½ inch sting with round-nose pliers. Now, pass the ear wire into the loop you formed earlier. At this point, you will

have a plain hoop earring. Now, repeat the procedures above for the second earring.

5. Get about 15 inches of the 24-wire gauge. Then, twist the wire string about four times around the hoop's end. As you proceed, add beads to the string. While feeding the string, follow this sequence—bead seeds, a double coned bead, and then, a pearl bead.

6. For this project, wrap the wire strings two times around the earrings, while going back and forth to spread the density. Cut off the excesses of the string with flush cutters.

7. If you wish to alter the shape of the earrings, you could go ahead with it. You are done!

Chinese Firecracker

Tools and materials

- 4gm of Vermilion red matte
- Japanese Delica beads (size 11.)
- 10 inches of Sterling silver chain.
- 42 sterling silver ball top headpins.
- 2 sterling silver shepherd's hook with ball ear wires.
- 6 sterling silver jump rings of 4mm diameter.
- Round-nose pliers
- Chain-nose pliers.
- Wire cutter.
- Ruler.

Procedures

1. Cut out four pieces of wire with each about two inches long.
2. Place a two-inch wire at the mouth of the round-nose pliers with one inch of wire at either side of the pliers.

3. Use your right hand to grip the pliers and then, cross the wire over each other with your left hand to form a loop. You can use this technique for the four-wire strings.

4. Use your left hand to grip the loop you just made before placing the pliers on the wire for the side loops. This technique will help the loop to be made neatly. The tip of your pliers will form a small loop while the bottom, a big loop.

5. Flip the wire and repeat the procedure above for the rest of the wires. To make this earring, the wire should be ¼ inches long.

6. Place the chain-nose pliers on a jump ring and then, pull one of the edges towards you.

7. Place a hold on the loop you have formed before you can move ahead to slide the earring into the loop.

8. Close the loop you formed by directing the pliers at the three o'clock angle. Afterward, push back the wire.

9. To make the firecrackers, fix nine Delicas on each of the thirty-eight headpins to create the dangly effect.

10. Fix five Delicate beads on each of the four headpins for the links that tie the decorative wire strings together. To form the ninety-degree angle, cut the ball from the bottom of the beads with round-nose pliers.
11. Turn the wire string from the top of the pins so that you can make loops on either side of the beads.
12. Measure the length of the wire you bent. See that it is about ¼ inches long before cutting it out. Repeat this procedure for the other four bead links.
13. Measure and cut out 1½ inch length of chain sections. Then, you can measure and cut out two inches of chain sections.
14. Fix headpins to the chain. For each 1½ inch length, thread about seven headpins. Then, for the two-inch sections, start at the end of the chain before going in an upward direction.
15. Fix the shapes of the chandelier together with bead links.
16. You can join the two inch chain to the central loops of the chandeliers with beads. For the two 1½ inch chains, use jump rings to attach each of

the side loops. Fix earring wires to the central loop of the chandelier shaped beads.

17. You are done!

Aquarius Necklace

Tools and Materials

- 1 aquamarine 15mm by 12mm of a rough-faceted nugget.
- 13 smooth aquamarine of a dimension of 8mm by 5mm Rondelles.

- 14" of sterling silver with a length of 3.1mm length.
- 26" of sterling silver with 22-gauge.
- 6" sterling silver with 20-gauge wire.
- 11.3mm sterling silver with a lobster clasp with a jump ring.
- 1 sterling silver bead cap. (7mm to 8mm)
- Round nose pliers.
- Flat nose pliers.
- Wire cutters.
- Liver of sulfur or stew wool.

Procedures

1. Cut out the three strings of the chain into four long links. Ensure that a short link remains at the end of the chain.
2. Cut out another string of chains to six different long links. You should also leave a short link at the end of the chain.
3. Cut out the 22-gauge sterling wire in pieces that are two inches long.
4. Wrap the three aquamarines together with the wrapped loop technique. Afterward, fix the two ends of the aquamarines to the four-inch-long

link bead. Now, wrap a string of three aquamarines around another chain. This procedure sets the central part of your necklace.

5. Add three aquamarines to each end of the center of your necklace. Then, join a three-link chain to one end and a six-link chain to the opposite end.

6. Use the last string of the 22-gauge wire to add a bead cap to an aquamarine. Then, you can wrap this structure to the end of a six-link chain. A lobster clasp will be at the other end of the six-link chain. To fix the clasp, use the jump ring fixed to it.

7. To attach the pendant to the necklace, use a six-inch length cutting of the 20-gauge wire to string the nugget. The nugget must be fixed to the center of a wire string. Now, turn the wire strings at either side of the nugget before twisting it around once.

8. Wrap the short end of the string across the knot you made earlier, then, straighten the long side. After then, wrap the short end of the string around it.

9. Create a loop on the long end of the string by following the wrapped loop technique. When you are done, cut off the excesses with a flush cutter.
10. You are done.

Cherry Cordial Cuffs

Tools and materials

- 50 feet round 24-gauge wire.
- 15 inch round 12-gauge wire.
- 6 strands of freshwater pearl.

- 13 brown keishi beads (7mm by 5mm)
- 22 garnet faceted Rondelles (6mm by 4mm)
- 13 champagne faceted rounds (8mm)
- 19 burgundy smooth Rondelles (5mm by 4mm)
- 19 bronze potatoes (4mm)
- 12 peach potatoes (7mm)
- Black marker.
- Ruler
- Mini file.
- Flat nose pliers.
- Round nose pliers.
- An oval bracelet mandrel.
- A bench block.
- A chasing hammer.

Procedures

1. Begin with the 24-gauge wire. You can use five feet of the wire first. Then, wrap the wire above the spirals that are at either end of the frame. Wrap the wire about five times.
2. Feed beads through the wire string until you get to a point where the frame is filled to an extent. Then, you can wrap the opposite side of the frame thrice.

3. Repeat the step above until you have the whole frame covered.
4. To finish the process, make five tight wire wraps.
5. You are done.

Bling Ring

Tools and Materials

- 21 Swarovski crystals (any color of your choice)
- 21 silver round beads (3mm)
- Ring with one, two, or three loops.
- Sterling silver with headpins that are 1½ inches long.
- Round-nose pliers.

- Chain-nose pliers.
- Side cutters.

Procedures

1. Fix one of the crystals to the headpin. Then, fix the silver beads to the Crystal's head.
2. Bend the wire above the final bead of the headpin through either the crystal or the silver bead.
3. Use the round-nose pliers to form a loop right above the bend, to form a complete circle.
4. Pass the end of the headpin through the groove on the bling ring. Continue to run the pin through the groove until the loop formed is within it.
5. To fix the dangles to the ring, hold the pin firmly against the groove with chain nose pliers. Then, use your other hand to wrap the pin's mouth around its bottom. You will see the wrapped knot exactly above the bend.
6. Twist the wires about three times, with each twist close to the previous. As you continue, try to pull the twists together to keep them secure.
7. Cut the excesses with a flush cutting tool. While cutting, place the tool close to the wraps and twists.

8. You can use the chain-nose pliers to press the end of the string flat against the wraps and twists. You can further get rid of any roughness along the string by running your fingers along it.

9. Repeat the procedure for the rest of the crystals, while separating the dangles evenly at every point the groove exists in.

10. You are done!

Rob Roy Cocktail Ring

Tools and materials

- 1 red miracle bead (red color)
- 1 brown miracle bead (brown)
- 5 glass fire-polished beads (4mm)
- 18-inch length of sterling silver (18-gauge wire)

- 4-inch sterling silver (22-gauge wire).
- Ring mandrel.
- Ruler.
- Wire cutter.
- Chain-nose pliers.
- Round-nose pliers.

Procedures

1. Cut the 18-gauge wire into three strings with each portion a length of six inches. You can grip the three wire strings at the central portion. It is at this point that you twist the 22-gauge wire.
2. Fix the 22-gauge wire to the central part before wrapping one if the ends twice to the right side. Then, roll the other end twice to the left side. Take note that you wrap the string in a direction away from the center.
3. Trim the excesses of the 22-gauge wire string with a flush cutter. Then, use chain-nose pliers to tug the twists of wire together.
4. Find out the size of your finger, i.e., your ring size. Then, wrap the 18-gauge wire to a size six.

5. You can hold the mandrel within the grooves of a vice. Then, use your fingers to wrap the wire string about it.

6. Twist the wire strings right in the front of the mandrel rod. This technique is similar to how you would knot a plastic bag. To keep the ring's shape, you can tug tightly at the knot.

7. To add the beads to the strings, go with one bead at a time. Then, you can keep the bead in place by instantly twirling the end of the wire string into a swirl.

8. Use the narrow edge of the round-nose pliers to bend the wire into a small circle, i.e., loop. This loop will be the center of the twirls you later use the string to do.

9. Hold the loop with your chain nose pliers. See that the wire strings face the left side of the pliers.

10. Tug the wire in a direction that faces you to begin the additional wire twirls. Use your left hand to open the pliers so that you can move the wire to the top. You can continue with this technique until you get to the part with the spiral. Just keep twirling the string until you get your ring size.

11. You are done!

Chapter 6

Fixing Wire Wrapping Jewelry Mistakes

Here, we will look at the mistakes you could make as a beginner and see how we can correct them or avoid them altogether.

1. **Non-uniform loops:** To avoid this issue, see that you mark your round-nose pliers with a permanent marker, scribing tool, or tape. For wire-wrapped loops, you could work with a ratio of two to one. For spirals, use a ratio of one to one. If you use a permanent marker, you might have to remark those points again when they eventually wear off. You could also get a 6-step multi-sized wire for looping jewelry pliers to cut out the stress and trouble.

2. **Incorrectly cutting the wire strings:** If you are making this mistake, then, you need to learn how to make use of your cutting tool. For cutting anything related to jewelry, the flush cutter is recommended. The tool has two faces—the one at the front, which is above the one at the back. If

163

you cut from the front, you will get a pinch cut. For a flush-cut however, you will need to cut with the back of the pliers.

3. **Opening jump-rings the wrong way:** You shouldn't open a jump ring by pulling the two ends apart. First, start by aligning the two parts of your plier so that the opening of the jump ring is at the topmost center. You could either use bent-nose pliers or a chain-nose plier for this step. Now, tug at the handles of the pliers with each of your hands going in the opposite direction, i.e., one heading towards you and the other, away from you. See that you are not pulling the ends apart! To close the jump ring back, do the opposite of all that was listed above.

4. **Tool marks along the span of your project:** Actually, the best thing to do to avoid marks left by tools is to use as few tools as possible. However, in cases where the tool marks occur, you don't have to leave it there. For slight scratches, file it slightly with a needle file. This file will make the metal look scratched, so, to get rid of that too, use a fine-grit jeweler's sandpaper. If the marks are deep, you might need to file the

string until it is thinner. But then, see that you are simultaneously filing both sides of the string.

5. **Issues caused by wire shaping:** As a beginner, you may redo some loops or coils. That alone can cause the string to get rough, but then, there's a solution. You could twist a 28-gauge sure string about the parts that have issues so that it can act as a kind of coverage. Apart from covering the mistakes, your project will have a better texture.

6. **Brittle wire strings:** Wire strings become brittle as you try to shake them, so, if you want them to be strong again, you could have them heated and cooled successively until you get the strength you desire of them. This technique will also go a long way to eradicate tool marks.

7. **Buying low-quality wire strings:** This is one of the costliest mistakes anyone could ever make. Low-quality strings could easily break or snap into two when the tension on them becomes too much. The bad thing here is that you might end up losing a tangible number of your beads. Each project has the gauge of wire it needs. Stick to it to avoid unnecessary issues.

The end... almost!

Hey! We've made it to the final chapter of this book, and I hope you've enjoyed it so far.

If you have not done so yet, I would be incredibly thankful if you could take just a minute to leave a quick review on Amazon

Reviews are not easy to come by, and as an independent author with a little marketing budget, I rely on you, my readers, to leave a short review on Amazon.

Even if it is just a sentence or two!

So if you really enjoyed this book, please...

\>\> Click here to leave a brief review on Amazon.

I truly appreciate your effort to leave your review, as it truly makes a huge difference.

Chapter 7

Wire Wrapping Frequently Asked Questions

1. What kind of wire is best for making rings?

Like it was said earlier, you get to know what wire is best for a particular project when it can be easily bent and at the same time remain as one without snapping into two. The best wire for rings though is the 22-gauge wire as it is a general-purpose wire.

2. How can a dead soft wire be hardened?

You can harden a dead soft wire by following many techniques. First, you can run the mouth of a nylon-jaw flat-nosed plier from one end to the other end of the wire string. You need to do this carefully so that the whole length is straightened out evenly. This technique works better with the thinner wire strings. You could also hammer the string with a mallet or a chasing hammer. However, before you begin to hit it, see that it is first placed on a steel bench block. Lastly, you could twist the wire string. This technique is only suitable for round wires as the other shapes will make the twists very evident.

3. **How can you wrap a stone without a hole?**

Align two strings of wire. Then, you can fix another string of wire that is about seven inches long across them in a vertical direction. Then, twist your vertical wire firmly about the horizontal strings about three times. See that none of the twists overlaps along the way. Then, pick up the right wire you just wrapped and then, pass it across one of the horizontal wires.

4. **What are the basic tools needed to start wrapping wires for jewelry?**

You will need craft wires, beads for decoration, flush cutters, round-nose pliers, chain-nose pliers, chasing hammers, a steel bench block, and a mandrel. Consequently, as you begin to try out other advanced projects, you could get other advanced tools and materials like jigs.

5. **What does the term, gauge, mean?**

Gauge is a term you will mostly see when you are seeking the right wire string to purchase. It is used to describe the relative thickness or thinness of a wire string. The lower the gauge number of a string, the denser it is, and the higher the gauge number is, the thinner the string will be. Lastly, know that the gauge of a wire is a measure of its width.

Conclusion

Now, we have come to the end of this outline on the art of wrapping strings of wire for jewelry and different kinds of ornaments. As a beginner, all you need to do is get the basic materials, and then, lay your hands on each of the projects discussed in the pages of this book. If you are not satisfied with how any of your project trials come out, do it over and over again until you get it. There's no harm in repeating something if it means you getting it. Then, you should study the possible mistakes listed in this guide so that you do not repeat them too. Certainly, if you can work with the right amount of patience, you would be able to head towards the level of professionalism in wire-wrapping.

Happy wrapping, artists!

CPSIA information can be obtained
at www.ICGtesting.com
Printed in the USA
BVHW041806281121
622723BV00027B/975